SUN GODS,
SERPENTS
AND
SLIPPERS

SUN GODS, SERPENTS AND SLIPPERS

Jamila Gavin

Illustrated by Diana Renzina

Collins

Contents

The Rose Slippers

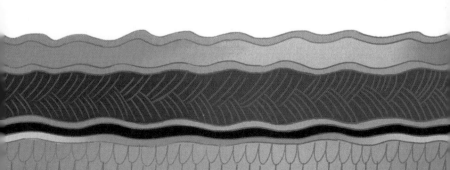

Ancient Egypt

Egypt is a country in north Africa.

Ancient Egypt refers to a time in history that spans 3,000 years, from 3100 BCE to 332 BCE.

Most people in ancient Egypt lived along the River Nile. They used the river for water, food and transport.

Ancient Egyptians made amazing constructions such as the Great Pyramids.

They created lots of paintings and sculptures that are still around today!

Gods and goddesses

The ancient Egyptians had more than 2,000 gods and goddesses!

We can see some of them in paintings that still exist. Lots of the gods and goddesses had human bodies and animal heads.

Ra: the Sun God

Osiris: the King of All Living Things

Horus: God of the Sky

Isis: Goddess of Motherhood

Nut: Goddess of
the Heavens

Anubis: God of
the Underworld

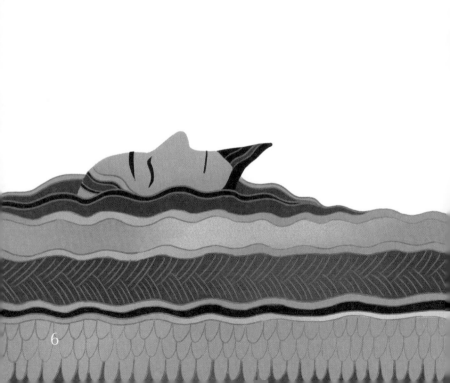

THE SECRET NAME
Chapter 1 Creation

Before the beginning, before creation, there was nothing. Nothing but a vast expanse of water.

Before the beginning, there was no name for anything because there was nothing, except the Great Watery Father, Nu.

Nu lived in the deep, dark, endless water which was also called Nu.

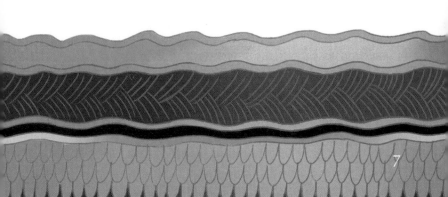

Then, from the very darkest depths of Nu, the Great Watery Father wanted light. So he began to think. Out of his thinking sprang a god which he called the Sun. Nu was pleased. The Sun was so powerful, Nu decided to give him more names. He called him Kepera at dawn, Ra at high noon, and Tum in the evening.

Ra at high noon was the most magnificent, and Nu called him the Great Thinker and the Great Creator. But there was one last name Nu wished to give Ra. It was a name so powerful, and so divine, that it had to be a secret name. It was so secret, even Ra himself didn't know it. Nu hid this glorious name deep inside Ra, where it would protect Ra from all evil.

After that, Ra reigned in the Heavens and on Earth.

Whatever Ra wanted to see, he only had to think of it and it was there. As soon as he saw it, he named it.

Whatever he thought of, deep within his great mind, it was there. And he named it.

When Ra wanted to create further gods, he thought so deeply that they leapt out from his mind. As soon as they appeared, he named them.

There was Seb, the God of Earth, and Nut, the Goddess of the Heavens. There was Shu, the God of the Wind, and Tefnut, the Goddess with the head of a lion. She was known as the Great Spitter, the Bringer of Rain.

When Ra wanted to see creatures of the land, and creatures of the sea and sky, he thought about them. Then, at once, they appeared, and he named them.

All of these creatures were born from his mind: the lions, monkeys, camels, cats and dogs; whales, sharks, octopuses, and stingrays; eagles, crows, nightingales and finches; spiders, bees, ants and scorpions. Ra created all of the creatures that leapt, crawled, fluttered, slithered, swam and flew.

And he created their habitats: forests, deserts, rivers and seas, and beautiful gardens bursting with flowers. What joy for the gods and goddesses who loved to bathe in waters scented with rose petals.

Ra was so pleased with his creation that, from his great shining inner eye, he thought about humankind. Then, at once, he took the form of a human. How he enjoyed walking with his gods among the humans he had created.

For many centuries, Ra and his gods walked upon Earth.

During this time, Seb, the God of Earth, and Nut, the Goddess of the Heavens, had a daughter who they called Isis. But Isis was not powerful enough to walk among the gods. She only walked among the mortals.

Although she had magic powers and was an enchantress, Isis craved more power and honour. She longed for the same power as the Creation gods and to be allowed to walk with them.

So, she decided she would discover
the secret name of Ra. Then she would be equal
with the gods.

Isis began to follow Ra.

Isis was there when Ra sat on his glorious throne and made laws. She was there when he wandered through his gardens, strolled by his rivers, or entered his dark forests. She was there when he sat in his sun boat and sailed the skies.

She followed him across all four corners of Earth, marvelling at his wonderful creation. Yet, she still did not discover his secret name.

As the centuries rolled by, Ra became old, and then very old. When he spoke, he dribbled, and this moisture trickled down his chin and fell on the ground. It was time for him to give up walking among mortals, and return to the Heavens.

15

Chapter 2 The secret name

All this time, the Enchantress Isis had been working on her magic powers, hoping to discover Ra's secret name. Suddenly, she realised she had one magic power that she hadn't yet used. She stayed close to Ra and watched when he rested and slept.

One day, as Ra dribbled with old age, his spittle fell to the ground.

Isis ran forwards. She blended the spittle into the earth, rolling it and kneading it. She used it to create one creature Ra had not thought of. It was a serpent. None of the creatures Ra had created had ever hurt him. But this creature, the serpent which Isis had made, contained a deadly poison.

She hid the serpent near a path where she knew Ra liked to walk. Then she followed Ra patiently. The moment would come.

One day, as Ra passed by, the serpent reared its head and bit him. A terrible burning poison entered his body. He fell to the ground, crying out in agony.

The gods heard him, and called out with worry. "What has happened to you, oh Mighty Ra?"

At first, Ra couldn't speak because of the trembling of his limbs, the chattering of his teeth and the rattling of his bones. He rolled in agony. He'd never known pain until now.

Finally, he called out: "Gather around me, all you gods and children that I have created! Chant over me the most powerful words that you have been taught, and perhaps you can save me."

So the gods all came – and so did Isis, the Enchantress.

For hours the gods chanted every word they knew, but nothing could soothe Ra's pain.

Then Isis stepped towards him.
"What is wrong?" she cried.

"Something terrible has poisoned me,"
he howled. "It burns my flesh, but is not fire;
it is not ice or water, yet it freezes my body.
My eyes can't see, and sweat falls from
my face."

"You have been bitten by a serpent," cried Isis.
"But, Great Ra, I know how to take away
your pain. Tell me the one secret name that you
received from Nu, and that none of the other
gods know. Tell me the name that you carry deep
inside you, which contains all your power. If you
tell me that name, I can save you."

Ra wept. "I created the Heavens and Earth.
I made the mountains and the sea; I cause
the River Nile to overflow and nourish the lands
of Egypt.

"When I open my eyes, there is light,
and when I close them, there is darkness.
But my secret name? I have no secrets. I am
Kepera at dawn, Ra at high noon, and Tum in
the evening." He did not speak the most secret
name that Nu had hidden inside him, because
Ra himself didn't know it.

"I can't help you then," declared Isis.
"You have still not given me the most powerful
name of all."

At last, tormented by his fiery pain, Ra raised his head and cried into the sky: "Oh Mighty One, oh Father, Great Nu! You have given me a secret name so that no evil could harm me. I beg you, give this name to Isis. Let it be carried silently from me to her."

At that moment, Ra vanished from the sight of the gods and of all living things. The sun boat was empty, and a dense darkness settled over the land. The secret name leapt from his heart and entered Isis.

Isis called out for the venom to leave Ra's body. "Now that I have his secret name, allow the Sun to lighten our darkness. Let Ra live again among his beloved mortals."

And so, the god Ra returned to his Earth and lived again. There was no longer any pain or sorrow in his mind or body.

He lived until his bones became silver, his flesh turned to gold, and his hair was the colour of true, dark lapis lazuli.

And Isis became the All Powerful.

Explaining the beginning

The start of the world is such a big idea that lots of stories have developed to explain it. We call these creation myths.

Lots of cultures through history and around the world have different creation myths that explain how the world and life began.

Egyptian god Nu
lifting a boat from
the waters of creation

Many ancient creation myths see water or the sea as the place where life started.

The story of the secret name of Ra starts with the very beginning, before creation. But even before anything else, there was water, and the God of Water – Nu.

Isis and Osiris
Chapter 3 The terrible trick

Osiris was a Human God.

When he came to Earth as a man, a voice from the Heavens cried out: "The Lord of All Things has come among humans. He will be a good and wise king."

Before Osiris, there was no peace among the people. Tribes roamed the land, fighting each other. There was no law or honour.

But when Osiris sat on his throne, a new age began. He created strong laws, and sat in wise judgement. Peace came to Egypt.

Isis, the Queen, ruled beside him. She was
a goddess of great wisdom; of learning
and healing. She knew how to cure the sick.
She knew how to make things grow. It was she
who turned the tribes into peaceful farmers.
She and Osiris showed them how to work
the land so that there was plenty of food.
Under their rule, Egypt became a land of
plenty; a land of milk and honey.

Osiris wanted to make sure his people were happy. So he travelled the length and breadth of Egypt, building temples and teaching people how to worship. He was greatly loved as he reigned without force, and always spoke with understanding. His land rang with music and happiness.

While Osiris was away visiting parts of his kingdom, it was Isis who ruled. She too was loved for her great wisdom.

But Osiris had a brother called Seth. Seth became more and more jealous of Osiris. Whenever his brother was away, he would scheme and plot to overthrow Osiris so that he could rule the land.

Seth wanted power. He wanted to stir up trouble in the kingdom. But every time Seth thought of ways to get rid of his brother, somehow Isis always stood in his way. She knew what Seth was thinking and what he wanted. She knew he loved war more than peace.

So, Seth decided he must use cunning instead of force.

Once, Osiris was due to return from a long trip. The cooks were ordered to prepare a feast to celebrate his homecoming.

There was much merriment when Osiris came home. When he entered the great hall, everyone was laughing and dancing. The musicians played their harps and pipes, and people lined up to present Osiris with gifts.

"I, too, have a present for Osiris," Seth cried out. He summoned his servants to bring in his gift.

Everyone crowded round in amazement. Seth laid before his brother the most magnificent chest anyone had ever seen.

It was made from the best ebony, and carved with mysterious designs.

Seth raised the lid and boasted: "I had this chest carved for one man, and one alone. Only he can fit into it exactly."

Everyone joked and lined up for a chance
to lie down in the chest and see if this was true.
One by one, they got in and stretched out.
But either they were too long, or too short,
or too fat, or too thin. "Go on, then!" they
challenged Osiris. "Now, it's your turn. Let's see
if you fit into this chest."

Full of smiles, Osiris leapt into the chest and lay down. Behold! He fitted perfectly. But before the cheers of triumph died away, Seth slammed the lid shut, nailed it down and padlocked it.

Isis rushed forwards in alarm. "Let him out!" she cried. "The joke is over." But followers of Seth surrounded Isis, and forced her away. They challenged anyone who tried to fight back or defend Isis.

Then Seth and his men heaved up the chest and carried it down to the Nile. They tossed it into the fast-running river, and watched it swirling away. Soon it disappeared into the darkness, and was carried far away to the sea.

When Isis heard what Seth had done, she wept in despair. She was going to have a baby, and now Osiris would never know his child. She dressed herself in clothes of mourning for her dead husband.

Grief-stricken, and on the run from her enemies, Isis fled the palace. She promised that she wouldn't rest until she had found the body of Osiris.

Chapter 4 Isis and the search

Now Seth ruled the kingdom. He spread cruelty and sorrow.

Day after day, Isis followed the River Nile as it flowed to the sea. Month after month, she searched, asking everyone she met: "Have you seen a chest floating in the river?"

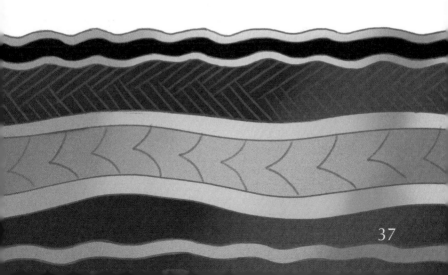

Near the Delta, where the river meets the sea, Isis met some children playing on the shore. "We saw a chest!" they told her. "The waves carried it into the open sea." Isis hurried to where they were pointing. Her eyes scoured the empty horizon. She wept because she could see nothing.

The followers of Seth were trying to track her down. They knew Isis was going to have a baby who could be a threat to Seth. So Isis often had to hide among the swamps and jungles of the Delta.

From Heaven, the god Ra saw the distress of Isis, and the danger she was in. She was now close to giving birth, so he sent seven giant scorpions to protect her.

One day, exhausted from her wanderings, Isis came to the door of a poor woman. She knocked, hoping to find shelter. The woman opened the door, but when she saw the fearsome scorpions, she screamed and slammed it shut.

Isis spoke to her gently. "I need your help. My baby is about to be born. I promise the scorpions won't hurt you." So, the woman let her in.

When Isis saw the woman had a sick child, she spoke special words, and gave her powerful herbs. The child quickly recovered, and the woman was so thankful that she welcomed Isis to stay as long as she needed.

And so it was that Isis gave birth to a son in this hut. She called him Horus.

One night, Isis got a message from heaven. "You must escape. The followers of Seth have heard about the birth of Horus. Seth is full of jealous anger. The throne of Egypt belongs to Horus, son of Osiris. Leave quickly. You and your baby are in danger."

Gathering her baby, Isis fled into
the darkness. She made her way to the city
of Buto. A goddess called Uazit lived there, and
Isis gave her baby to Uazit for safekeeping.

Once more, Isis continued her search
for Osiris.

Isis went to the land of Syria. There, she heard of a king who had created a sacred pillar from the trunk of a mysterious cedar tree. The tree had sprung up around a chest which had been washed up on the shore. Isis was certain this chest contained Osiris.

She begged for permission to cut into the trunk and take out the chest, so that she could carry the body of Osiris back to Egypt.

The king gave his permission, and gave her a ship to sail up the Nile.

When Isis reached Egypt, she hid the chest deep in the jungle, and hurried back to Buto to find her son, Horus.

Seth was out hunting in the jungle, and by chance, came across the chest. He recognised it at once. He dragged the chest to the river, and flung out the body of Osiris to be eaten by crocodiles.

However, the crocodiles wouldn't eat this sacred body, and it floated away.

Once more, Isis went looking for her husband, Osiris. She would never rest until she had found him. Year after year, Isis searched until, at last, she came upon his body.

Joyfully, she transformed into her goddess shape: a winged spirit. Her fluttering wings stirred the air as she hovered over Osiris. Isis breathed air into his mouth, and gave him life.

And so Osiris departed from this Earth to become Lord of the Underworld.

Osiris was now the Great Judge and King of the Dead. His son, Horus, known as the Falcon God, defeated his wicked uncle Seth in battle, and finally reigned on the throne of Egypt.

When Isis died, she was reunited with Osiris in the Great Hall of Truth, and they lived for ever in the Field of Reeds, where streams flowed and fruit trees grew.

Isis and Osiris around the world

Isis and Osiris from the great temple of Seti in Egypt

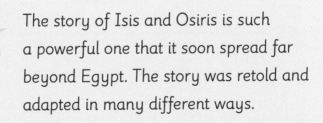

The story of Isis and Osiris is such a powerful one that it soon spread far beyond Egypt. The story was retold and adapted in many different ways.

The goddess Isis was worshipped in different places. Her fame spread to Greece and Italy – and even as far as Britain.

a Roman statue of Isis

Historians have found proof that there was a Temple of Isis in London nearly 2,000 years ago! It might have looked like the one here, in Spain.

The Rose Slippers

Chapter 5 An unexpected gift

Rhodopis was a beautiful girl, with a kind heart, dark, glimmering eyes, long chestnut hair, and skin as soft as a rose petal. Everyone called her Rose.

Rose lived with her mother and father, but they were very poor. Her father was a fisherman, so he was often away at sea for days on end. Her mother worked hard, trying to make enough money to put food on the table, by stitching and mending clothes. But life was hard. Rose's mother hoped that Rose's great beauty and loyalty would make it easy for her to find a good, rich husband. "Your face is your fortune," she would say, stroking her daughter's rosy cheek.

One day, Rose's father fell ill, so he could no longer go on long fishing trips. "I can't afford to feed you any more, Rose," he told her sadly. "You must go out and look for work."

So, Rose went to the market place to see if she could find work, but it was useless.

She wandered sadly down to the shore to sit and dream und watch the waves. Suddenly, she was surrounded by robbers who took her aboard their ship. They would take her to a market place in Egypt where they knew they could sell her for a good price.

One day, Rose stood in the market place, full of sorrow and homesickness. An elderly man called Charaxus came by. He was just passing the time – he hadn't intended to employ another servant. He had enough for his household. But his eyes were drawn to the sad girl, with chestnut hair, and rosy cheeks.

"I'll take her!" cried Charaxus, and the deal was done.

As Charaxus walked home with Rose, he wondered if his wife would be furious. After all, he'd paid a lot of money for a servant they didn't really need.

At first, his wife was very cross, and gave Rose all the hard jobs to do around the house. But Charaxus noticed that Rose never frowned or sulked.

He saw that she was cheerful as she went about her duties, and she was always singing. Not only was she a willing worker, but she delighted in feeding the birds and squirrels, and herding the geese. She talked to all the animals as if they were her friends.

Rose's sweet nature made the other servants jealous. Because Rose was so keen and ready to help, they secretly bullied her.

"Look at little goody-goody! Master's pet and little treasure. Such lovely rosy cheeks, but let's make them even more pink!" And the other servants pinched Rose's cheeks until they were red raw.

One day, on his wife's birthday, Charaxus held a party. There were tables groaning with food, and musicians who beat drums, tinkled bells, clashed cymbals and played the pipes.

Everyone at the party gave the mistress of the house a gift. Rose had made a posy of flowers. It was a beautiful floral gift, collected from the fields nearby, and tied up with string. But the other jealous servants found it and, gleefully, destroyed it. So, when the servants all lined up, one by one, and laid their gifts before the mistress of the house, Rose stood back with empty hands.

"Well?" demanded Charaxus. "Nothing from you, Rose?"

Rose stammered. "I … I didn't have anything worthy enough," she said, with tears in her eyes. "I thought perhaps I could dance for you."

Charaxus waved at the musicians. "Play!" he commanded. "Give her a chance. Let's see how well she dances."

The drums beat, the cymbals clashed, the bells tinkled and the pipes played. Rose began to dance. How beautifully she swayed and moved. Her arms flowed with grace, and her feet hammered with the rhythm of the drums. Everyone was enchanted by her skill and elegance.

Even Charaxus's wife sighed with pleasure. "You're right, dear husband, Rose is a treasure. I'll sew her some dancing shoes to make her happy." So she stitched Rose a pair of rosy slippers, edged in gold thread.

They were the most beautiful slippers Rose had ever seen, and from that hour onwards, she was never without them.

Chapter 6 If the shoe fits

The gift of the beautiful rosy slippers made
the other servants even more jealous of Rose.
One day, when Rose went down to the River
Nile to bathe, she left her rose slippers on
the shore. One of the meanest of the girls crept
towards the slippers, to steal them. Just then,
a falcon flew down from a high tree and
snatched one of the slippers away.

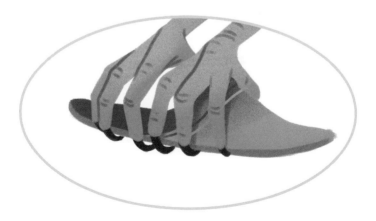

The falcon was none other than Horus –
the god who had one eye which was the Sun
and the morning star, and the other eye which
was the moon and the evening star.

Horus was the son of Isis and Osiris.

With the rose slipper in his beak,
the falcon flew and flew. He made his way
along the shining blue Nile until he reached
the king's palace.

King Amasis was holding court, sitting on his golden throne in the shade of cooling palms and fruit trees. The falcon flew overhead, hovered, then dropped the single rosy slipper onto the king's lap.

The king was astounded. He held the rose slipper in his hands, staring at it in wonderment.

"Where is the other slipper?" he asked everyone. "Who can find the girl who owns the second slipper?" He had to know.

As it was a falcon who had given him the slipper, Amasis knew it was an omen from Horus. He made a solemn announcement. "I will seek out the woman whose precious foot fits this slipper. I feel sure we are meant to be together."

Messengers were sent all over Egypt.
They went from door to door asking if anyone
owned a single rosy slipper with gold threads.
But no one did.

At last, a messenger came to the door
of old Charaxus. It had become a house of
sadness since his wife died. Only Rose made
him smile when she danced or sang for him,
and baked him the cakes he loved best.

The messenger asked all the girls of the household if they owned a single rosy slipper with gold thread. Every girl received the same query, whether rich or poor, whether a daughter or a servant.

"I had a pair of rose slippers," cried a girl. "But I lost one, and threw the other away as it was now useless."

"I have a rose slipper, but I've mislaid it," cried another.

One by one, the girls claimed that they had once owned a pair of rosy slippers, stitched with gold thread, but somehow, they couldn't find them.

No one could produce a slipper.
The messenger turned towards the doorway,
ready to leave. He asked one more time:
"Have I questioned every girl in
the household?"

"Yes! You've asked us all!" they cried,
knowing full well that Rose, who had been left
in the kitchen, hadn't been asked.

"You haven't asked me," said Rose,
quietly coming forwards. "And I have
the other slipper."

She drew from her robe a single rosy slipper
with golden thread.

Charaxus watched with sadness as Rose
left with the king's messenger. He was sure he
would never see her again, and tears fell from
his eyes.

Rose arrived at the king's palace.
When Amasis met Rose, he fell in love with
her kindness, and loyalty, and her rosy cheeks.
He asked her to sit down and put on her
rosy slipper. Amasis then held out the other
slipper which Horus, the falcon, had dropped in
his lap.

She slipped it on, and it fitted perfectly.

"This is surely a sign that we are meant to be together," proclaimed the king, joyfully.

There was to be a marvellous wedding, and Rose asked if Charaxus, whom she loved like a father, could attend.

Her wish was granted. What is more, to make Rose happy, the king commanded that Charaxus should be given his own house nearby. There he could live until the end of his days, and Rose could visit him whenever she wanted.

So, they all lived in great happiness.

The story of Cinderella

Does the ancient Egyptian story of the rose slippers remind you of anything?

Can you think of another story where a poor girl loses a shoe and ends up marrying a prince?

There are different versions of the Cinderella story in almost every language in the world!

Researchers think there may be more than 800 versions of the Cinderella story going back thousands of years!

What might a modern telling of Cinderella be like?

Cinderella from 1849

a film version of *The Story of Tam and Cam*,
a traditional Cinderella story from Vietnam

Hieroglyphics

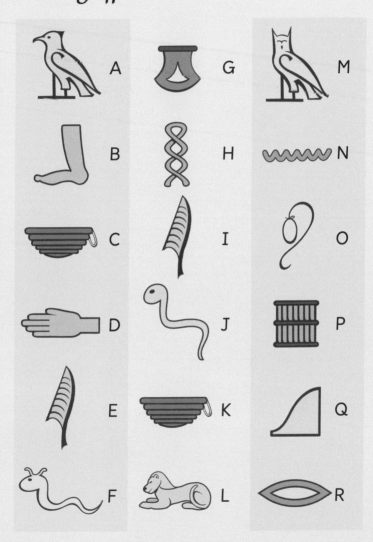

A

G

M

B

H

N

C

I

O

D

J

P

E

K

Q

F

L

R

S

V

Y

T

W

Z

u

X

| 1

|| 2

||| 3

|||| 4

||||| 5

6

7

8

9

∩ 10

∩∩ 20

∩∩∩ 30

9 100

1000

About the author

A bit about me …

My name is Jamila Gavin. I live in Stroud, England, but was born in India, and lived there for much of my childhood. I learned to love world myths and legends from an early age.

Jamila Gavin

How did you get into writing?

I discovered that many children, especially from diverse ethnicities and backgrounds, didn't know about their own stories. I wanted to write for them, and inspire them to write stories too.

What do you hope readers will get out of the book?

I hope they will be excited by marvellous ancient stories about Creation and gods, but also see what other cultures and religions have in common with each other.

What is it like for you to write?

It is a continuation of a passion for reading, writing and storytelling that I have always had from childhood. I love both the freedom of inspiration, and the daily routine of sitting down at my desk to write.

What is a book you remember loving reading when you were young?

Before I could read, I loved ghost stories – if only looking at the illustrations and being frightened to death.

But as soon as I could read, it was fairy tales and myths and legends that I loved, and still do.

Why did you want to write this book?

Ancient Egypt fascinated me: so old, so extraordinary, yet so wise. The more I read their myths and legends, the more connections I saw with other religions like Hinduism, and even Christianity.

Which of the three stories in this book do you like best, and why?

For me, all three are part of one long story, so it's hard to choose just one. I've always loved Creation stories, and this one, starting in water, does remind me of the Hindu Creation story which also starts in water.

What place do you think myths have in the modern world?

I wish more people knew them, to realise their wisdom, and to realise more deeply how cultures have changed over time. We have so much more in common than divides us.

Have you ever been to Egypt?

Yes, I have been to Egypt. My trip was far too short, but I grabbed the chance in case I never got another one. But I would love to go again and visit places I couldn't get to before. I know Egypt has had a grip on the imagination of so many people, not least Alexander the Great, and the amazing Roman historian, Herodotus.

About the illustrator

A bit about me …

My name is Diana, I live in Riga, Latvia, and I work as a full-time illustrator.

Diana Renzina

What made you want to be an illustrator?

An illustrator can tell stories through beautiful images.

How did you get into illustration?

As a child, I liked to draw illustrations for my books. When I grew up, I learnt that this was a real job!

What did you like best about illustrating this book?

Egyptian art and mythology are very distinctive, so it was very interesting for me to immerse myself in this world.

Is there anything in this book that relates to your own experiences?

Although this book is mostly about gods and goddesses, these stories are also about feelings. Feelings such as envy, grief, fear and happiness, which I, like everyone else, also experience.

How do you bring a character to life in an illustration?

I bring a character to life though colour, expressions and posture mainly.

Which of these Egyptian stories do you like best? Why?

I like the first story best. I love how poetically it ends.

Did you have to do any research to illustrate these stories? What did you find out?

I did! I found out that landscapes in Egypt can look very different – from deserts to beautiful seascapes.

Do you think ancient Egyptian stories are still meaningful for people today? Why?

I think they definitely are. If we leave the mythological element and the gods and goddesses, what remains is a story about human feelings and relationships.

Book chat

Had you heard
of myths before
reading this book?

What did you know
about ancient Egypt
before reading this book?
What have you learnt?

If you could change
one thing about this
book, what would
it be?

If you had to give
the book a new
title, what would
you choose?